P9-CDK-540

Let's Investigate with Nate

Written by Nate Ball Illustrated by Wes Hargis

The Water Cycle

HARPER
An Imprint of HarperCollins*Publishers*

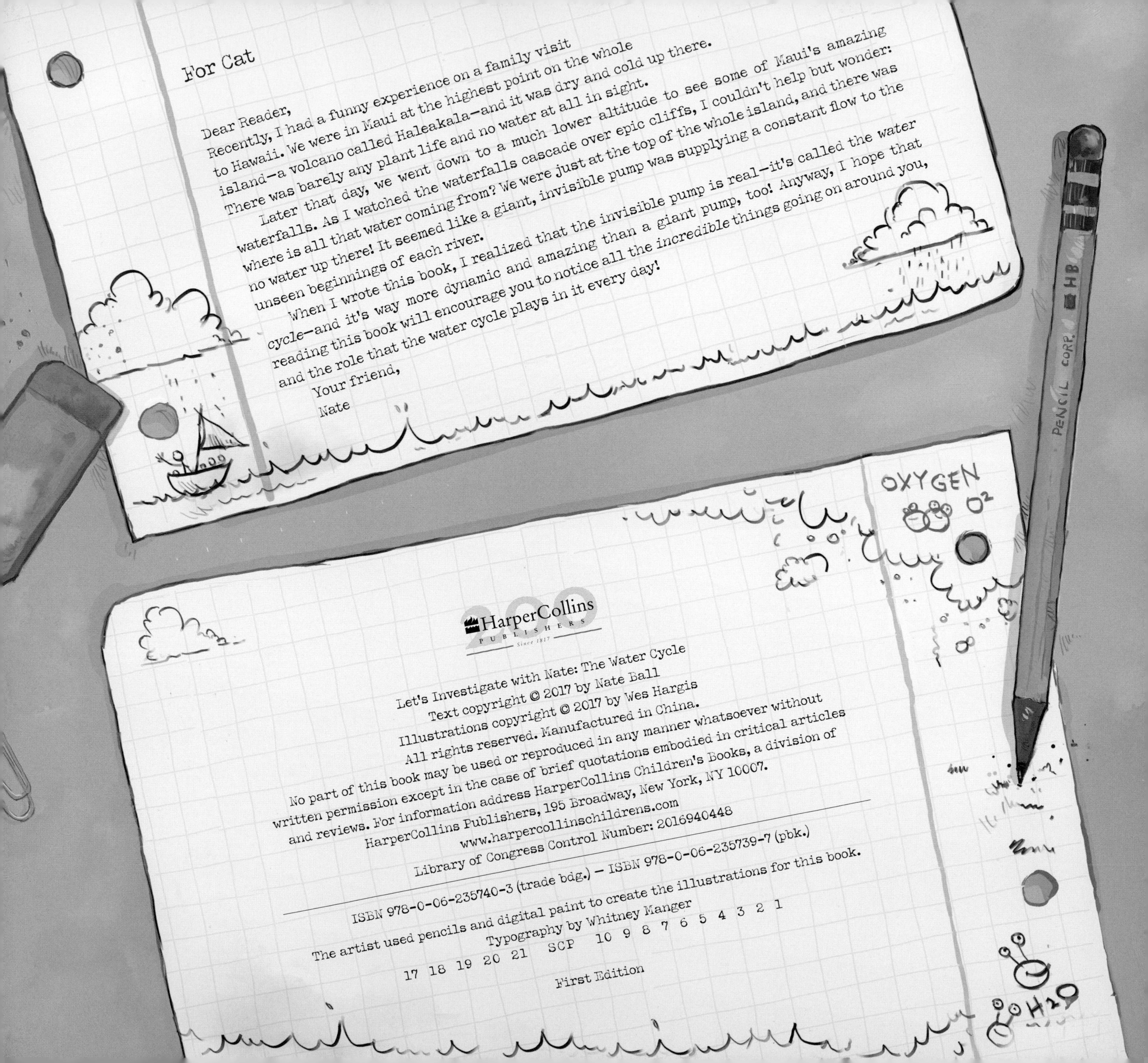

For Cat

Dear Reader,

Recently, I had a funny experience on a family visit to Hawaii. We were in Maui at the highest point on the whole island—a volcano called Haleakala—and it was dry and cold up there. There was barely any plant life and no water at all in sight.

Later that day, we went down to a much lower altitude to see some of Maui's amazing waterfalls. As I watched the waterfalls cascade over epic cliffs, I couldn't help but wonder: where is all that water coming from? We were just at the top of the whole island, and there was no water up there! It seemed like a giant, invisible pump was supplying a constant flow to the unseen beginnings of each river.

When I wrote this book, I realized that the invisible pump is real—it's called the *water cycle*—and it's way more dynamic and amazing than a giant pump, too! Anyway, I hope that reading this book will encourage you to notice all the *incredible* things going on around you, and the role that the water cycle plays in it every day!

Your friend,

Nate

HarperCollins Publishers
200
Since 1817

For information address HarperCollins Children's Books, a division of HarperCollins Publishers, 195 Broadway, New York, NY 10007.
www.harpercollinschildrens.com
Library of Congress Control Number: 2016940448
ISBN 978-0-06-235740-3 (trade bdg.) — ISBN 978-0-06-235739-7 (pbk.)

The artist used pencils and digital paint to create the illustrations for this book.
Typography by Whitney Manger
17 18 19 20 21 SCP 10 9 8 7 6 5 4 3 2 1

First Edition

MUSEUM
OPEN
AT
10 AM

The Science Museum opens at ten a.m. on Saturdays. That's when most people get to come inside. At ten a.m., the Science Museum is a normal museum. But in the hour before it opens, something special happens. Every door in the museum becomes a portal to another world . . . and those doors open only for daredevil scientist Nate Ball and a special crack team of curious kids.

Hi, Investigators!
Ready for some fun
and adventure?
Private Wendy, ready
to learn!
Hi, Braden!
How are you
today?
You're late,
Felix.
It's already
9:01.
What are we investigating today?
I hope I know some of the answers.
I'm sure you'll
do great, Rosa.
The answers are
waiting for you
to find them!
NATE

HALL OF WATER
Are you guys ready to learn about the water cycle? You're in for a wild ride!
Yeah, we're ready!
The water cycle? What's that?
I hope we don't get wet.
I hope we get really wet!
HALL OF DINOSAURS
HALL OF LIFE
Here are your tickets. Each ticket has a question for you to explore.

Today's investigation is all about water. The **water cycle** is the way water moves from the sky to the ground and back again. You don't always notice it, but there's water moving around you all the time—even in the air!

Let's see what Braden's science journal has to say about cycles. . . .

BRADEN'S JOURNAL

A cycle is a bunch of steps that are repeated in the same order. For example, a laundry machine's cycle starts with water. Then it mixes in soap, then it rinses the soap out. Then you get your clothes dirty again, and you do the laundry all over again. That's a cycle.

HALL OF STARS
I always do my own laundry.
My dad does mine.

Do you know the answers to these questions?

Great job! But that's just the beginning. You each have one more question on your ticket. In order to answer these questions, you'll have to do some serious investigating.
What kind of water lives in the sky?
What causes evaporation?
What causes water droplets to form in the air?
When is a river hidden from the sky?
NATE

SATURDAY
9:07 A.M.
Okay, Investigators! Remember– science is all about exploration! So pay close attention to everything around you. We have to learn about the water cycle before 10 a.m., when the museum opens to the public!
We have to find the answers to our tickets in less than one hour?
Yep! The museum turns back into a normal museum at ten!
Hey, look, we're flying!

But if we're here to learn about water, why are we in the air?
NATE

Air is transparent. You can see right through it. But that doesn't mean there's nothing in it. Air is made out of **molecules**, which are so small you can't see them. But if you could see them, you'd see that they are always bouncing around and crashing into each other!

BRADEN'S JOURNAL

A **molecule** is a group of **atoms** that are bonded together.

An **atom** is a tiny building block of all the stuff we have in the universe—**solids, liquids, gases,** and **plasmas.** That stuff is called **matter.** There are different kinds of atoms—we call them the **elements.** You've probably heard of some of them. Iron is an element. Helium is an element.

Oxygen and **hydrogen** are both elements.

When two hydrogen atoms bond with an oxygen atom, you get a molecule. Not just any old molecule, either—a water molecule!

What are you doing up in the air?
Shouldn't you be down on the ground, in a lake or something?
When I'm in a lake, I'm liquid. But right now, I'm gas!
Now I know what kind of water lives in the sky. I have the answer for my ticket!
Awesome job, Wendy! That's one down and three to go.
NATE
Water Vapor

When water is solid, it's **ice**. When it's liquid, it's **water**. When it's gaseous, like the air, it's water **vapor**.

This water vapor is all mixed up in the air. Water vapor is also called **steam**. You can make steam by boiling water on your stove!

BRADEN'S JOURNAL

You know how a traffic light is always either red, yellow, or green? The color of the traffic light is the "state" that the traffic light is in.

Well, molecules have **states** too. A molecule can be in a solid, a liquid, a gas, or a plasma state. (A plasma is like a special kind of gas that mostly happens in stars.)

How come we aren't all falling down to the earth? How come we're just bouncing around in the sky?
We're super small right now—as small as a water molecule. The air underneath us is acting like a cushion!
So . . . we're not big enough to fall?
Yep. That's called air resistance, and it's awesome! Take it away, Braden!

BRADEN'S JOURNAL

Air resistance just means how the air pushes against you when you move through it. Air resistance is why a kite stays in the air when you run with it. You're pulling on the kite but the air is pushing on it. That's what keeps it up high.

When something is very, very small (like a single water molecule), it only takes a tiny push from the air to move it around.

So a single water molecule stays in the air because the air pushes it up harder than gravity pulls it down.

But something bigger than a water molecule might be heavy enough to fall through the air.

Earth's atmosphere is mostly made of nitrogen and oxygen. "Atmosphere" is a fancy term for the mix of gases that surround a planet. Here on Earth, we have a special name for our atmosphere: we call it "air."

Brr!
That's a cold wind.
It's getting pretty chilly. What do you see happening to the water?
It looks like the molecules are cuddling up with one another.
Sharp eyes, Braden!
Yes! I have the answer for my ticket! What causes water droplets to form?
The molecules get cold and want to huddle together.

When it gets cold, the water molecules huddle up close. They all pack together tight in little groups. Each little group is a **droplet**. The water molecules are now in a liquid state. They aren't gas anymore.

If a water droplet gets big enough, the cushion of the air beneath it can't hold it up anymore. Then it becomes **precipitation**, which is water that falls to the Earth's surface.

Hold on tight! We're in a rainstorm!
You got that right! THis is the fun part! Yee-haw!
Oh good, this is how the water cycle starts!
We're falling!
We're falling! Whee!
Watch out, ground! Here we come!
Incoming!
PUDDLE
STREAM

When rain falls from the sky to the earth, it often forms **puddles**. These puddles can trickle downhill until the water reaches a **stream**. And that stream may lead to a **lake**.

The lake has a **dam** at one end. But it lets some water through into the **river**, down at the bottom of the dam.

An **estuary** is the area where a river flows into the ocean. The freshwater of the river mixes with the salty water of the sea. And when the tide comes in, the estuary flows backward!

Water flows back and forth with the tides in an estuary. But eventually the water ends up in the ocean. And so have Nate and the Investigators!

The water in the ocean doesn't stay still. The ocean has currents that are always moving. These currents sweep Wendy, Braden, Felix, Rosa, and Nate far out.

These water molecules are really wiggly!
We don't stop bouncing around when we're liquid, you know.
Yeah, we just bounce slower and closer together!

BRADEN'S JOURNAL

Remember that cold wind that made the water vapor turn into rain? That was a current, too. Wind is just another word for "air current." So a water current is like a water wind!

It's a hot, sunny day. The sun is shining on the ocean. The water right at the top of the ocean is getting warm. The warmer it gets, the harder the water molecules bounce off each other.

Some of them bounce so hard that they bounce right back into the air—and become gas again!

This is called **evaporation**.

Ugh! I'm too hot!
Ah! It's much better in the atmosphere!
It's great to be a gas . . . and be in the air again.
Oh my gosh! Now I can answer the question on my return ticket! What causes evaporation?
Nice job! Now we just have to find the answer to Braden's ticket before ten a.m.!
Hey, I can find the answer to my own ticket, thank you very much.

Energy, like heat, makes water molecules move faster, until they bounce from a liquid to a gas state.

Now that everyone is back in the sky again, an air current comes and sweeps them back to shore.

Nate gave the kids four return tickets for this investigation. Each ticket had one question on it, remember? Well, three of those questions have been answered.

As the air cools down, the water molecules slow down. They aren't bouncing around as fast anymore.

The water vapor molecules gather close again. It keeps getting colder! The molecules are getting less and less wiggly . . . and more and more sleepy.

The cold takes all their energy away.

The water molecules are **freezing**! As they freeze, they pack very close together and form ice **crystals**. These crystals gather more and more molecules into them and get bigger and bigger. Soon, each crystal can be seen with the naked eye.

It doesn't take long for each crystal to become a single **snowflake**.

The question on my ticket is about rivers. I think that means we have to get back down to the ground.
It's a good thing we have a snowflake to ride with. Hang on tight! This is going to be awesome.
Hop on, cowboys!
Yee-haw!

The sun comes out again. Its warmth gives energy back to the water molecules, and the snowflakes begin to melt. Now they're becoming liquid again.

As the sun shines, some of the water molecules bounce around so hard they turn right back into gas, and rise up into the air.

But other water molecules have a different idea. They soak down into the earth.

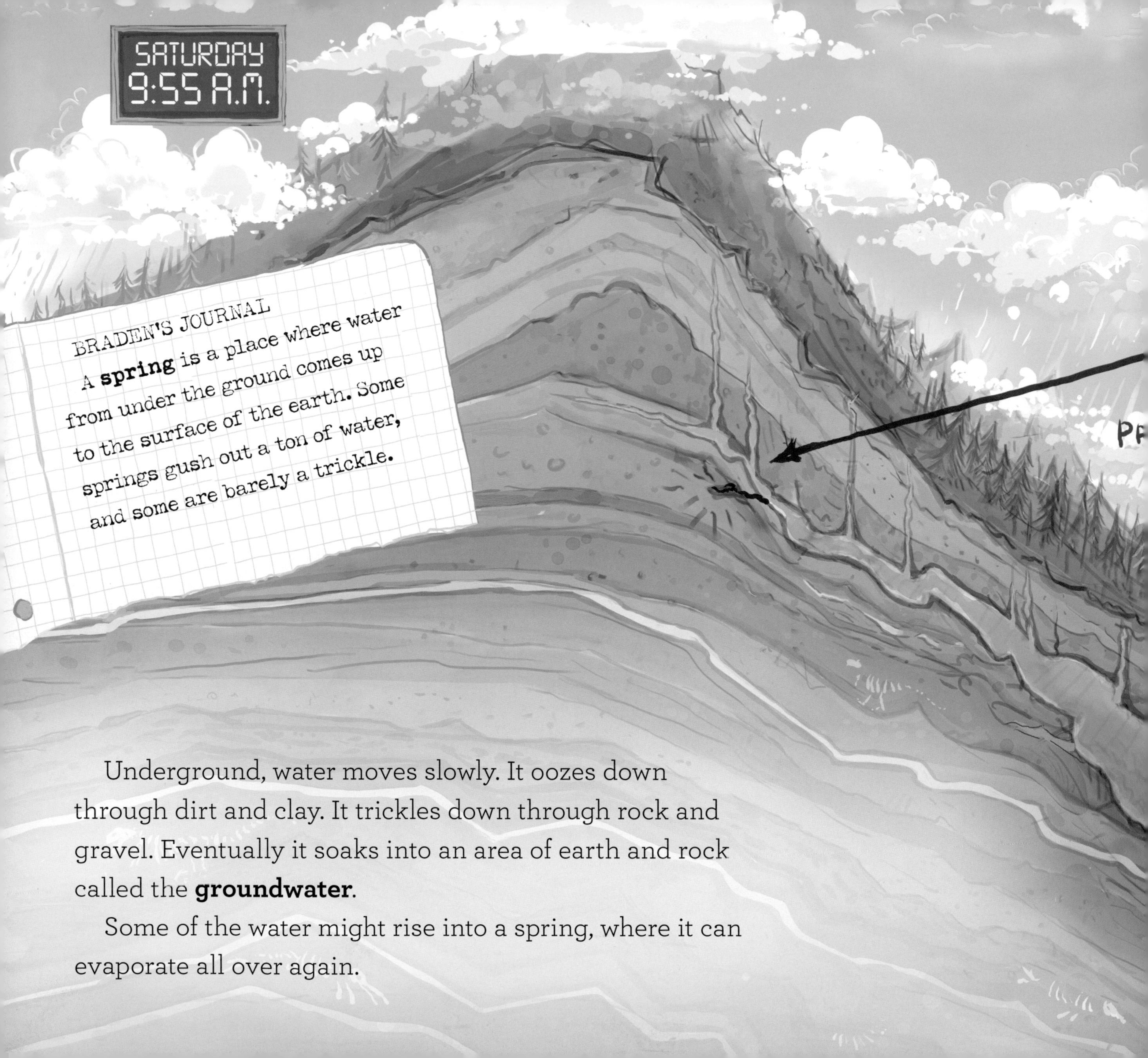

SATURDAY
9:55 A.M.
BRADEN'S JOURNAL
A **spring** is a place where water from under the ground comes up to the surface of the earth. Some springs gush out a ton of water, and some are barely a trickle.

Underground, water moves slowly. It oozes down through dirt and clay. It trickles down through rock and gravel. Eventually it soaks into an area of earth and rock called the **groundwater**.

Some of the water might rise into a spring, where it can evaporate all over again.

All of this can take a really, really long time.
How long? Months?
No, years. Can you believe it?
ITATION
If the museum goes back to normal while we're still here, we'll be trapped!
We don't have years! The museum opens in five minutes!
WHEN AM I GOING TO FIND THE ANSWER FOR MY RETURN TICKET?
SPRING
GROUNDWATER
When is a river hidden from the sky?

A **subterranean river** is a river that runs under the surface of the earth. Often these rivers run through caves. Because the water doesn't evaporate, it can stay in these underground rivers for years.

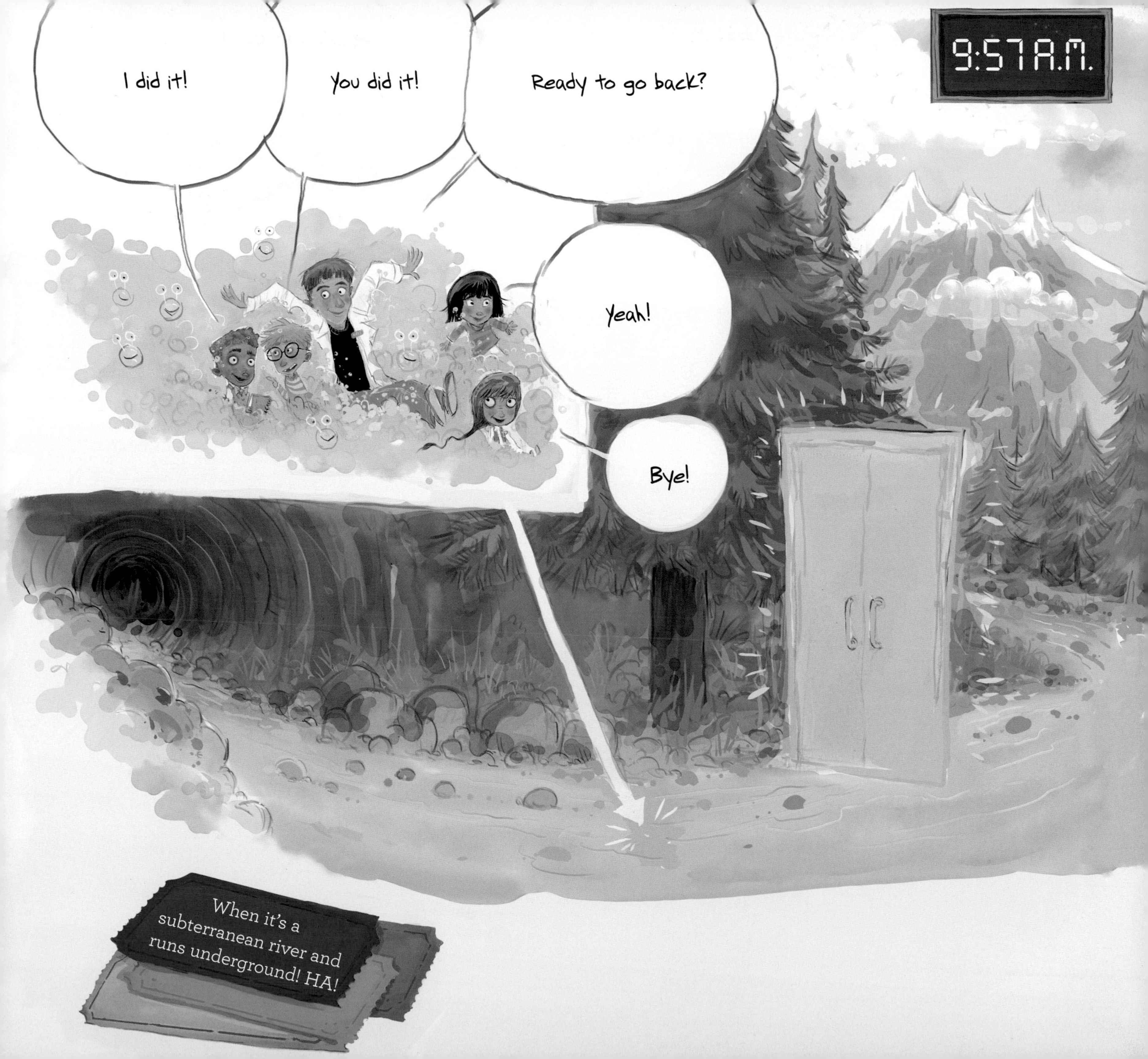
9:57 A.M.
I did it!
You did it!
Ready to go back?
Yeah!
Bye!
When it's a subterranean river and runs underground! HA!

9:58 A.M.
The Science Museum!
POP!
That was an excellent adventure!
We're back to our regular sizes again!
Now you guys know all about the amazing water cycle!
I can't believe I didn't figure out my ticket sooner.
NATE

This adventure is complete! The Investigators found the answers for all four return tickets . . . just in time. The Science Museum opens in two minutes, and that's when all the doors go back to normal.

This week's investigation is over. But don't worry—Nate and the Investigators will be back soon for another adventure!

Important: Do this experiment with the help of an adult!

Experiment: Make Your Own Cloud

Wouldn't it be cool to make your own cloud? In this experiment, we'll see if we can figure it out!

For the sake of learning some of the "how-to" of science, let's pretend that we don't actually know how cloud formation works. How would we go about discovering how clouds really form? We'd investigate using the scientific method:

1. Make observations about the world around you.
2. Form a hypothesis (an idea) about how you think something works.
3. Design an experiment to methodically test your hypothesis.
4. Analyze the results of the experiment, enhance your understanding (hypothesis confirmed or not?), and possibly repeat the whole process, learning more each time!

Let's use that method for clouds!

1. From the book and in real life, you may have made these observations:
   Observation 1: Clouds often form over where water has been evaporating, like over the ocean. This means that water vapor is close by.
   Observation 2: Clouds usually form high up in the air, where the temperature is colder.
   Observation 3: Even when we can't see it easily, all through the air there are tiny particles like pieces of dust, smog, smoke, and even salt crystals above the ocean.
2. Based on these observations, you might form the following hypothesis:
   "I hypothesize that clouds form by combining water vapor, cold air, and tiny particles like dust or smoke."
3. To test whether this hypothesis is true, you'd design an experiment that will allow you to combine those three ingredients!

The Experiment:

You will need:

- an adult (important!)
- a thick glass jar with smooth sides that you can easily see into
- black paper to cover half of the jar
- tape to hold the paper on
- a bag of ice
- boiling (or almost boiling) water, enough to fill the jar about 1/3 full
- a book of matches

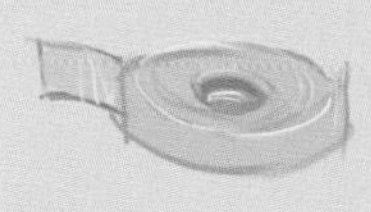

Step 1: Tape the piece of black paper around the jar so that half of it is covered from top to bottom and the other half is clear. That's the backdrop—you'll view through the clear side.

Step 2: Pour the boiling water into the jar and swish it around a bit.

Step 3: Have an adult light a match and hold it over the jar for a few seconds. Then drop the match into the water.

Step 4: Plug the top of the jar with the bag of ice and watch closely what happens inside the jar!

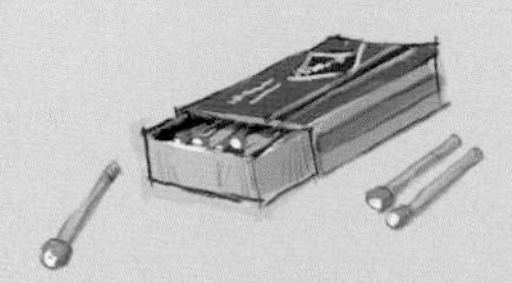

Let's get the results!

What did you observe from the experiment? Did a cloud form? What does that say about your hypothesis? Was it correct?

Remember, even a well-designed experiment can take a few tries to work well. Don't be too frustrated if you don't see clouds right away—instead, ask, "Is there something I can do differently, or could do better?" Keep at it! Change one thing at a time and keep trying till you're confident in your process. Getting the process right is a big part of science.

Last, remember to keep going! What other things do you wonder about the world? What have you observed, and how might you design an experiment to test your new ideas? Get out there and try it, Investigators!

–Nate

GLOSSARY

ATOM
An atom is the smallest unit of matter, or the physical stuff of the universe. These tiny particles are too small for the eye to see.

CRYSTAL
A crystal is a solid material, and it is made of atoms (or molecules) that are arranged in a regular pattern. Quartz is a crystal, and so are snowflakes.

DAM
A dam is a barrier that stops water from flowing freely. It is usually built to keep water in one place. Dams can also help create electrical power, using the weight and flow of the water to drive generators.

DROPLET
A droplet (also known as a drop) is a very small blob of a liquid (like water). Droplets can be formed when vapor is cooled so that the vapor atoms come together into liquid form. When this happens with water, the droplets can become clouds, fog, or rain.

ELEMENT
An element is a pure chemical substance. An element is made entirely of a single type of atom. All matter in the universe is made of the elements! Water is not an element, but it is made out of two elements in combination: oxygen and hydrogen.

ESTUARY
An estuary is a place where a river or stream meets the ocean.

EVAPORATION
Evaporation is when a liquid turns into a gas. This can happen when the surface of the liquid vaporizes into the gas touching it. It can also happen extra quickly when a liquid boils! A pot of water will evaporate if it's boiling or if it's just sitting out in a dry room.

FREEZING
Freezing is what happens when a liquid reaches the temperature where it turns from liquid to solid. The atoms or molecules gather together very tightly when they are solid.

GAS
Gas is a state of matter. Atoms are very energetic when they are in the gas state and bounce around a lot, with lots of space between them.

GROUNDWATER
Groundwater is water beneath the surface of the earth. Unlike a subterranean river, the water in groundwater doesn't move very fast . . . in fact, sometimes it hardly moves at all.

HYDROGEN
Hydrogen is an element. Hydrogen atoms are one of the elements that make up H_2O . . . or water! Hydrogen is also the simplest and most common element in the universe. Stars are mostly made of hydrogen, and it makes up three quarters of the matter that exists!

LAKE
A lake is a body of water surrounded by land. It's larger than a pond . . . and it usually contains freshwater (unlike the salty oceans).

LIQUID
Liquid is a state of matter. Atoms are at medium energy when they are in the liquid state. They move around, but they are packed more tightly than when they are gas. Liquids have a definite volume, which means they take up a certain amount of space, but have no defined shape like solids do.

MATTER
Matter is anything that has mass. There are four states of matter—solid, liquid, gas, and plasma.

MOLECULE
A molecule is a group of two or more atoms that are held together by chemical bonds. The atoms in a molecule can be the same element as each other, or different elements.

OXYGEN
Oxygen is an element. It is one of the two elements that combine to make water, along with hydrogen. Oxygen is super important to most life on Earth, including humans.

PLASMA
One of the four basic states of matter. Plasma is like a liquid but is produced at high temperatures in stars and the Sun. It can result from a strong electrical current such as in lightning or neon signs.

PUDDLE
A puddle is a small pool of water on the surface of the ground. Usually puddles are formed from rain or from melting snow. Puddles evaporate into the air and eventually make rain clouds, or they soak into the ground and feed the groundwater.

PRECIPITATION
Precipitation is any form of water that falls from the sky. It can be liquid water (drizzle, rain, and mist) or frozen water (snow, sleet, and hail).

RIVER
Rivers collect water from the earth around them (and from precipitation) and carry it toward lakes or oceans as gravity pulls them downhill.

SNOWFLAKE
A snowflake is an ice crystal (or a blob of ice crystals) that forms in the sky and falls to the earth as precipitation. Snowflakes are created when microscopic droplets of water in a cloud freeze, and then grow by the process of "deposition"—where additional molecules of gaseous water go straight from a gas to a solid as they attach to the frozen droplet. When they do this, skipping the liquid state, they build up the special crystal structures that we love about snowflakes.

SOLID
Solid is a state of matter. When a substance is in its solid state, it is at its lowest energy. The atoms (or molecules) group very closely together and hardly move at all.

SPRING
A spring is where water from underground flows up to the surface of the earth.

STATE
The three most common states of matter on our planet are solid, liquid, and gas. There is also a special fourth state of matter called "plasma", which can be seen in places like lightning bolts, neon signs, laser tubes, and stars.

STEAM
The gaseous state of water, formed when water is above its boiling point 100°C (212°F).

STREAM
Streams are bodies of moving water similar to rivers but smaller and often much shorter.

SUBTERRANEAN RIVER
A subterranean river is a river that runs under the surface of the earth. Often, these rivers run through underground caves.

VAPOR
Vapor is a type of gas that condenses easily.

WATER
Water is a common substance made of two common elements: hydrogen and oxygen. Its chemical symbol is H_2O, because water molecules are made of two hydrogen atoms (two Hs) bound to a single oxygen atom (O). Water is found on Earth in all three of Earth's most common states of matter: as a solid (ice), a liquid (water), and a gas (steam/water vapor).

WATER CYCLE
The water cycle describes the way water moves across, above, and below the surface of the earth.